Our Butterfly Flies Free

The Brilliant Life Story of a Little Girl with Special Needs

Marlena Howerton

Inspiring Voices®
A Service of Guideposts

Inspiring Voices books may be ordered through booksellers or by contacting:

Inspiring Voices
1663 Liberty Drive
Bloomington, IN 47403
www.inspiringvoices.com
1-(866) 697-5313

ISBN: 978-1-4624-0396-7 (e)
ISBN: 978-1-4624-0395-0 (sc)

Library of Congress Control Number: 2012921226

Printed in the United States of America

Inspiring Voices rev. date: 12/21/2012

Contents

Our Little Butterfly has come Home

Looking across the green grass of a warm summer day, a butterfly lands on a rock and takes a look around. "Yes," says the butterfly, "I like it here. I think I will stay for a while." No one could have dreamed how much influence this decision to stay would have on so many, or how many blessings would be delivered by this angel, sent to encourage and bless the lives of all she came in contact with!

Sitting in church was becoming increasingly uncomfortable that blessed morning. The labor pains were getting too close together. Getting up itself was an ordeal, but the time had now drawn near. Arriving at the hospital, our blessing was almost ready to enter her new world. An hour and a half later, she was in position to be born. Just as my water broke and time had come for delivery, she turned. The doctor scheduled an immediate C-section and proceeded to deliver our beautiful angel to us. My baby girl was born August 31, 1991, in Tyler, Texas. This blessing that arrived would come to be named Alyssa.

When our precious little one came into this world, we had the anticipation and hopes of all young parents. Little did we know what a special gift we were about to receive. The glorious day of her arrival soon took a turn that changed our excitement and joy to confusion. Our day became dark and gray with concern. "No, no … not my baby! I don't understand! What is this spina bifida and hydrocephalus?" Alyssa had the most serious form of spina bifida: myelomeningocele. In this form, the backbone and spinal canal is not closed before birth. My sweet Alyssa's hips were terribly bruised and battered from the birthing process. Seeing her, my heart sank as I was told of her condition. After being anointed and blessed by our minister, the doctor took away our newborn angel. I knew it was for the best, but it was so hard to see her go with the medical staff. . Due to having a C-section, the doctor would not allow me to leave the hospital until I recovered from surgery. Grandma Jane and Alyssa's Dad went to Children's Hospital in Dallas, Texas to be with Alyssa. I could not let Alyssa be in the hospital alone. All of our family was at the hospital with Alyssa. Our friend Beth and many other friends went to Children's Hospital to be with Alyssa until I could be there.

After four long days, I was finally out of the hospital and able to travel to see Alyssa. Children's Hospital in Dallas, Texas, became our new home for a while. The doctors explained to us what operations Alyssa would need and what to expect now and in the future if she survived. "Please, please," I pleaded, "fix my baby!" Doctors explained they were unable to repair the nerve damage, but they could close her back. But doing anything at this time would be very dangerous for Alyssa. She had lost weight and would have to at least regain her birth weight before anything could be done.

It took a week for Alyssa to gain the weight necessary for this first surgery. The doctor didn't really give us much hope: "Take her home, and give her all the love you can." The medical team explained how to administer the catheter and how to give her suppositories to help her potty regularly. This was the top priority before I could take my Alyssa home, as she was paralyzed from the waist down.

An appointment was made for her in two weeks. The doctors were open and honest with us and did not expect Alyssa to make it to that first appointment. Chances were she would go to sleep and not wake up before that critical two-week period elapsed.

A very strong little girl was present and accounted for at that two-week appointment. Alyssa was now strong enough to have surgery to put a shunt in her head to relieve the fluid pressing on her brain. Two months later, they were able to go in and close her back. After a long recovery period, we were able to go home again. In our preparation to leave the hospital, one of our many nurses gave me this poem titled "Heaven's Very Special Child" written by Edna Massionilla. This poem talks about the blessings of caring for a special needs child. Why I was chosen for this special job of being Alyssa's Mom I do not know, but what I do know is that I am glad that I was. Stronger faith and richer love is something that I didn't understand when I read that poem. But I knew from the beginning that I was going to give Alyssa much love and a happy life. What I didn't realize is how rewarding my life was about to become as a result of being given the privilege of being Alyssa's Mother. What a joy and a blessing she has been to me.

The Journey Begins: Not Realizing the Depth of the Meaning of that Poem

Getting back to normal—whatever normality our lives would have. My getting back to work was a must so I could keep my medical insurance. Grandma Jane kept Alyssa while I worked. Our angel was five weeks old when Grandma Jane started keeping her, yet she had already undergone a major surgery. Grandma Jane played and talked with her throughout the day. She made many home videos and captured every little moment. Alyssa was clearly her pride and joy. Our butterfly was such a happy baby, always laughing a lot. She was a good baby, always sleeping through the night. Even as an infant, Alyssa always had a great temperament. I never thought I could love someone as much as I love my new baby girl.

At about six months old, we knew something was wrong again. Our normally pleasant baby had begun to cry much more, so I took her to the doctor. They admitted her and did a series of tests. The doctors said she wasn't getting enough oxygen through her blood and had to stay in the hospital for a week while she was given blood and monitored. When she went home, she did incredibly well and bounced back to the same bubbly little girl as before.

Also around this time, we noticed her eyes were crossing. The doctor tried using the patch method to correct it, but it was not successful. Nine-month-old Alyssa needed surgery to uncross her eyes. This was a very successful surgery, and her eyes were now perfect. She always had such beautiful eyes; they were chestnut brown with long, dark eyelashes. Her little face was so precious. It was perfectly round, but there was a small problem. As we looked at her face, we noticed her forehead was not forming correctly.

On their first birthday, most babies have cake all over their face and are surrounded by family and friends. On Alyssa's first birthday, she had cranial facial surgery to reshape her forehead. Her forehead was growing pointed due to the shunt that had been previously put in. And fluid on her brain was causing her skull to swell. So back to Children's Medical Center of Dallas we went. The surgeons cut her from one ear to the other, pulled back the flap of skin, and took off her skull. They shaved the bone in the middle of the forehead and added to the two sides of her forehead to make it even and smooth across the top. Then they put the skull back in its proper place. She was in ICU for a couple of weeks. What a first birthday! But as always, Alyssa was strong and resilient. The doctor explained to me how to remove the stitches after a couple of weeks. The surgery proved to be very successful; the doctors did an excellent job. The doctors thought she might need to have a second surgery on her forehead as she got older, but she never did.

Alyssa recovered remarkably from this surgery too and again proved to be a very happy little girl. She was our miracle child, always so strong and such an inspiration to me and everyone she came in contact with. She was a very energetic little girl and would go everywhere, scooting across the floor. At a little over one year of age, she was given a standing frame to stand in; this would help with the circulation in her legs. Her uncle Mike made her a custom-made pink table that was level with her standing frame. This allowed her to stand and play with her toys on her table. She would laugh and clap her hands and was always such a happy child.

Our angel's aunt Annette is a teacher and is always interested in spending lots of time with Alyssa as well as teaching her. During her early years, our butterfly would spend many hours with her aunt, playing and learning her numbers and colors. She also loved just talking to her aunt. Alyssa learned to speak well at a very early age. These two always had so much fun as they learned and shared so many new experiences. The knowledge Alyssa gained was so important as she advanced on her journey.

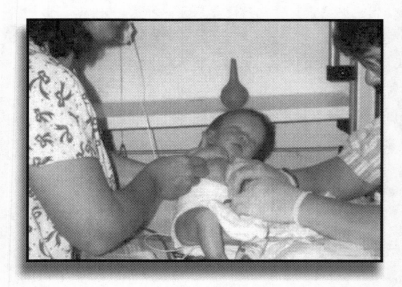

Alyssa started day care at Children's Place. She loved going to day care. New friends and lots of things to learn this made her so happy. The miracle had begun, and Alyssa was strong and determined. Our butterfly continued to grow, but problems were never far away. At about two years of age, we noticed one of her legs was red and swollen.

She had a spider bite on her leg, and it was swelling. The doctor treated her for it, and the bite got better. But the swelling did not go down. We took her back to the doctor, who did an MRI. It showed she had broken her femur. It had apparently happened a week before, and the femur was already knitting back together. In order to cast the break, the doctor would have to break the bone again. It was growing in position, so it was monitored twice a week to make sure it healed. Due to this, Alyssa could never straighten her leg completely.

With all of the surgeries and medical problems and procedures Alyssa had, she never failed to amaze us. Alyssa was always such a fighter, yet a strong and happy little girl. She set a perfect example of love by just being herself. She endured all of this and was so brave.

At this time, Alyssa received her first wheelchair and quickly learned how to use it. She always preferred sitting in her wheelchair rather than on the sofa. Her wheelchair was her legs, and she liked to be on the go. It surprised us all by how quickly Alyssa mastered the use of her wheelchair.

About a year later, she started school at three years old through Early Childhood Intervention, which she loved. Alyssa attended Bell Elementary that first year of school. Alyssa loved being around the teachers and other kids immensely. I think she enjoyed it so much because she was an only child. By age four, we were contacted by the Ambucks Organization from Longview, Texas, that does programs for special needs children. They wanted to donate a bicycle to Alyssa for Christmas and write a story for the local TV station. Alyssa accepted this wonderful gift, and within a few days, she was featured on the 5:00 and 10:00 p.m. local news broadcast, riding her new bike and smiling from ear to ear.

Our angel, Alyssa, never met a stranger and had the most outgoing personality. She made many friends wherever we went. She had a large vocabulary and enunciated her words perfectly from when she was very young. She could even say big words such as "ridiculous"; it was so cute hearing her talk. As Alyssa got older, she was known as a master conversationalist. Alyssa always had such a sweet soul.

At age four, Alyssa started Rice Elementary School and was a student in a mainstream classroom until fifth grade. The Early Childhood program moved from Bell Elementary to Rice Elementary. She made friends easily, and all the students wanted to push her wheelchair. As a matter of fact, the teacher had to create a schedule, so the students would not argue about whose turn it was. She loved going to Rice Elementary and liked all of her teachers. It was a good school, but the school system could never provide everything the special needs children needed. She loved all of her teachers, but her favorite during these early development years was Mama Sue. She would fix Alyssa's hair and sometimes babysat on weekends. There was always so much love between these two!

While at Rice Elementary School Alyssa took music. She played a recorder in her music class which she loved. She was always singing too and had a strong, outstanding voice. Alyssa also got the chance to be in a Christmas play in which she played the part of being a mouse. She did an excellent job. It was the cutest play and she was adorable. She was very enthused about this. After all she was a Drama Queen.

Her school activities always kept Alyssa very busy. She went on many field trips and was learning so many new things. Alyssa really got excited when the field trip was to the zoo. She was such an animal lover. Horseback riding was one of Alyssa's favorite things to do. She would sometimes ride horses at her grandma Jane's farm, too. Alyssa's love of animals had now begun to be very apparent.

Never lacking for things to do, our butterfly always had many extra activities of a various nature. Alyssa's church life had begun about age two, when she attended a Catholic church with her daddy Dave and me. Alyssa always loved going to church. She attended many church activities and especially enjoyed attending vacation Bible school with her friend Staci. They would go all week in the summer. At the end of the week they did a little show for parents and friends to come see (Staci was like a big sister to Alyssa). Alyssa also participated in the "blessing of the little children" when she was young. Alyssa believed God would protect and bless her always.

She was involved not only at church but with many other associated activities available to her. Between the ages of five and seventeen, she played Buddy Ball every year during April and May. She loved Buddy Ball. Aunt Marie, Uncle Mike, Cousin Cassi, Grandma Jane, and her friend Staci were her buddies for this program. They would push Alyssa's wheelchair around the bases after she hit the ball. She also played and enjoyed basketball and always wanted to go practice at the YMCA, where she also took swim lessons for years. The basketball games were always played at a local church. Alyssa also tried piano lessons, but she was not real fond of the teacher. Alyssa needed a caring and a loving teacher. Her teacher was not, so we moved on to something Alyssa enjoyed more. As you can see, Alyssa stayed busy at home, at church, and at school, and with many family activities.

At age three or four, it was again time for a surgery. This time it was to allow her bladder to open directly through her belly button and drain into her diaper. This worked great until she was older and larger, when her natural growth caused the diaper to no longer cover her belly button. It seemed the doctors and surgeries were never very far away. When Alyssa was seven years old, we had her bladder enlarged and had appendico-vesicostomy surgery, which was required to allow her to cath more easily. It looked like a second belly button that went into the bladder. This made it easier for Alyssa to cath herself. This proved to be a very successful surgery, yet she did get bladder infections from time to time.

When Alyssa was about nine years old, she had kidney stones. She had so many that the doctors had to do another surgical procedure to remove them. Laser surgery was not an option due to the number of stones. As always, she recovered fine from this and was enjoying life once again and never complained. She had a love for life and lived it to the fullest. Alyssa always had such a feisty spirit.

One of our butterfly's favorite things to do was to spread her wings and travel to new places, have new adventures, and, of course, make new friends. During the summer of 2000, Alyssa had her wish granted to go to Disney

Marlena Howerton

World in Orlando, Florida. It was truly a dream come true for her. Grandma Jane, Grandma Diane, and I accompanied her and also enjoyed this trip very much. Our butterfly was nine years old at the time and was granted this trip through the Make-A-Wish Foundation. Alyssa's wish for this trip and all the privileges it included was granted by this fantastic organization and handled in a professional manner by everyone involved. This was her wish come true and an incredible trip with so many exciting moments.

They flew us first class from Dallas/Fort Worth to Orlando. We were met by clowns at the DFW Airport to see us off. They gave us a mini-van for the week, tickets to all four parks, and spending money. During our visit, we stayed in Kissimmee, Florida, at Give Kids the World housing resort, which is like a small community in itself for the families of their guests. They always had breakfast and dinner for us at the Candy Cane House in Kissimmee, and the characters were always on hand to entertain us. The resort was also complete with a train, a merry-go-round, and a large pool for all the kids staying there to enjoy. There was also a nice chapel for the guests. Our accommodations were in a house that could sleep nine people and we were there for eight full days and nights. We went to Magic Kingdom four days. Alyssa rode every

14

ride she could get on and some she rode over and over. She rode Thunder Mountain eight times, it was her favorite. Alyssa was not scared of any of the rides. While at the park, Alyssa wore a special button so that all of the characters would know she had been granted a wish, and they would come over and talk and joke with her. There were no waiting in lines, because special needs children were taken to the front of the lines. She wanted to watch the Disney character parades every day and one day while watching the parade they were square dancing and one of the guys got Alyssa and her grandma Diane to dance in it with them.

One day we met Gold Dust Gus, and Alyssa thought he was crazy. He grabbed her wheelchair and started pushing her through the park. He yelled, "Here comes Alyssa," over and over so people would clear the path for her. Alyssa said this embarrassed her, but I think she loved it.

Alyssa was so privileged to spend her ninth birthday at Disney World. She had a character birthday party with dinner, and all the characters were there. The party was huge, and she loved every minute of it. The characters gave Alyssa a huge Mickey Mouse doll, and all of the characters signed it. They sang "Happy Birthday" to her and made a train pushing her all over the restaurant singing and dancing.

One night when we were going back to our house, we missed our turn and went almost to Tampa, FL. We ate dinner that night about midnight and got to bed around 1:30 a.m. Alyssa found this whole experience extremely comical, although it was somewhat frustrating to the remainder of our group. She always found the humor in things and made us laugh all the time. She slept at the restaurant, so by 8:00 the next morning, we were back at the park.

Our butterfly completely enjoyed Universal Studios in Florida and seeing where they make a lot of the movies. Alyssa got to see Barney, Baby Bop, B. J., and Mr. Peek-a-Boo. Alyssa also got to meet Barney and sing to him. She sang every song they sang on stage and acted out the songs with these characters. Alyssa was adorable! Some of the characters were so touched by Alyssa that they were crying. After the show was over, they had Alyssa hang back. They brought Barney out to see her, and she sang "I Love You, You Love Me" to Barney and took pictures with him. She was the most animated little girl singing at the Barney show. I can still see her smiling face sing that song with Barney. It was the cutest thing you would ever see.

We spent one day in Florida at the beach, because Alyssa wanted to play in the sand. She had so much fun it wore her out. She actually took a nap on the beach with me after she was finished playing in the sand. We ate dinner at the Rainforest Restaurant, which was very nice. Wherever she went, Alyssa made everyone laugh. Sometimes she was so busy entertaining that she couldn't eat. She loved to joke and laugh with people whether she knew them or not. She melted the hearts of people everywhere she went. She loved to travel and had the opportunity to go to many different places, but this trip to Florida was one of her most memorable ones. It was surely a dream come true for Alyssa.

Alyssa was always such an open person and always said what she thought without holding back anything. Her family and friends loved that about her. It never failed to amaze us how strong she was. Despite all of the surgeries, she was always positive and happy.

We owned a sporting clay range and had many types of events and shoots. We held benefit shoots; some were for Make-A-Wish, and several were organized for children with cancer. Alyssa needed a special desk in her classroom, but the school said they could not afford to supply it. We held a fund-raiser to raise money for her class each year while she was at Rice Elementary School. This allowed the class to have more books and the ability to take more field trips. And, of course, Alyssa got her nice, huge desk that her wheelchair fit under. Owning the sporting range was a blessing.

Alyssa enjoyed spending time at the sporting range and made many new friends there. One of those friends she became very close to was Jerel Morton. He was like a grandfather to her. Jerel had no other family and started hanging out with me and Alyssa. Jerel became like our family and is a very special person to us. He would always buy Alyssa a nice piece of jewelry for her birthday and Christmas. Jerel was there many times to help me with doctor appointments. He met us at the doctor when Alyssa had leg surgery and Jerel helped me get her out of the van. Several times he came to Dallas to see Alyssa when she was having surgery. They love to tease and joke with each other. Jerel loves Alyssa like his own granddaughter: they are very close. Alyssa and Jerel go shopping, out to lunch and sometimes to see a movie, a true grandpa.

Alyssa was always the life of the party and wanted to be involved in everything. She enjoyed being with her larger extended family, too. Her grandma Jane and I were always there with Alyssa when she had surgery. Grandma Jane spent many hours with Alyssa, listening to music and singing together, especially old classic country and gospel music. Alyssa knew all of the words to the songs and would belt them out loudly—and with all of the hand gestures to go along with them.

Country music was always a huge part of her life. Some of Alyssa's favorite singers were Alan Jackson, Dolly Parton, Loretta Lynn, Neal McCoy, Randy Travis, George Straight, Tammy Wynette, George Jones, Conway Twitty, and gospel singer Gloria Henson. She particularly loved Alan Jackson's music and was always listening to it, especially "Itty Bitty," "Small Town Southern Man," and "Bologna on White Bread." I bought Alan Jackson tickets when he came to Tyler, Texas, and she went to his concert. There was no way she would miss seeing him when he was in our area. Before the concert, Grandma Jane and I went into the sponsoring radio station to get some information about it. Grandma asks if it might be possible for Alyssa, a huge Alan Jackson fan since she was a small child, to meet him at the concert. Amy, from the radio station, worked things out for Alyssa and Grandma Jane to go backstage to meet him. Meeting Alan Jackson was a special memory for Alyssa. She was so excited about going to this concert and told everyone. It was an indescribable thrill for her. Alyssa has the book written by his wife, Denise, and an 8×10 picture of Alan. On one of Alyssa's visits to Alabama, she stopped and ate at Sprayberry BBQ in Newnan, Georgia, where Alan Jackson worked when he was younger.

Alyssa was blessed to meet several famous people throughout the years. Among them was Neal McCoy, whom she met when he was performing in Longview, Texas. Alyssa had her picture taken with him holding her in his arms. She met his sister, Barbara, and his mom and dad. She gave them hugs that melted their hearts. Neal's sister Barbara worked for Alyssa's Pawpaw Rick. As we have said before Alyssa was not shy and ask Barbara to take her back stage to meet him. Alyssa was in heaven. Neal regularly Hosts and performs at The East Texas Angel Network for special needs children.

Alyssa was also privileged to meet several sports heroes. She met Shawn Bradley, the basketball player, and did a commercial with him for Texas Scottish Rite Hospital in Dallas. Alyssa was amazed at his height. She would always say, "He is 7 feet 6 inches tall, wow!"

Alyssa's grandma Jane was so important in her life and development in many ways, but especially when it came to her music and religion. She was always such a positive influence in her life. One of Alyssa's favorite things to do was go to church and sing with Grandma Jane. She sang a solo at a church social once. The song was Alan Jackson's "Itty Bitty." For a Father's Day tribute, Alyssa and Grandma Jane sang "Farther Along." She sang this with great enthusiasm, putting all of her energy into it. It was beautiful, and the audience was so inspired. Some had tears in their eyes. Alyssa would also sing a song Grandma Jane sang when she was a child. It was called "How Far Is Heaven." Alyssa loved to sing this with Grandma Jane and sang it with her family in Alabama at Aunt Lena's eightieth birthday party in October, 2011.

Once Alyssa discovered her family in Alabama, she wanted to go visit anytime someone went that way. It was her all-time favorite place to visit. If anyone talked about going to Alabama, Alyssa was always ready to go, too. She was five years old when she took her first trip to Alabama. I remember Alyssa saying after her first trip there, "Why didn't you tell me about my wonderful family there?" When she was little, there was a special large chair Alyssa liked to sleep in at Aunt Lena's house. She just loved hanging out with all her cousins and Aunt's. Alyssa loved just sitting on the porch talking to everyone.

Sometimes it was a challenge getting into some of the family's homes, because they had steps and large porches with no ramp. But we always managed. One time our cousin Bobby created a ramp so we could push Alyssa's wheelchair up onto the porch. Alyssa was so appreciative to him. He quickly became one of her favorite cousins. Another cousin, Jimmy, would stop by and take out Aunt Lena's trash. Alyssa referred to him as the trash man, until she realized he was also her cousin. She enjoyed teasing and joking with her many cousins in Alabama. On one trip to Alabama, Alyssa went camping with family at Lake Garnerville, in northern Alabama. Alyssa enjoyed swimming in the pool there with her cousin Sheena and being outdoors in the beautiful countryside with its beautiful scenery. She thought it was fun sleeping in the camper, too. Alyssa went to numerous family reunions while on the family visits to Alabama. This was her favorite thing to do, because Alyssa got to meet so many family members. She kept in touch with her family in Alabama by telephone and through Facebook. If a family member was sick, Alyssa would call and check on him or her regularly. She had a deep concern for people when they didn't feel well. She was very close to her aunts, uncles, cousins, and other extended family members in Alabama. Alyssa would tell each one of them they were her favorite. She just could not help it since she loved them all so much.

Alyssa's life was full and rich with our immediate family, extended family, and community. But our butterfly could not be limited to just our little world. Being shy was not in Alyssa's vocabulary, especially in relation to meeting new people, having new experiences, and having it all written about. She was in the newspaper when she was nine years old for her Make-A-Wish trip to Florida. Alyssa was also on the front page of the newspaper for shooting a ram on a hunt at Laguna Vista Ranch in Kerrville, Texas. This trip was sponsored by the United Special Sportsman Alliance and Bridgett O'Donoghue. She was front-page news of a Louisiana newspaper when Alyssa met the LSU football team at the Scottish Rite Hospital. There was even an article written about Alyssa when she went to Wisconsin on her bear hunt.

Alyssa had the opportunity to go to several camps throughout the years. The first overnight camp that Alyssa went to was Camp Tyler in Tyler, Texas when she was about 6 years old. They mostly did arts and crafts. Alyssa did get the chance to ride the Zip line while at this camp. Our child was not afraid to try just about anything. Beginning around age ten and until she was sixteen, she went to Camp John Mark, which is sponsored by Texas Scottish Rite Hospital. I would take her to the hospital and meet with the pharmacists. All of Alyssa's medication had to be labeled and readied for the trip. They had all the medical necessities at this camp; a nurse and a doctor were there, too. Alyssa and the other kids enjoyed arts and crafts, water gun fights, and horseback riding. I still have all of the things Alyssa made at camp. A formal dance was always held on the last night of camp. Alyssa loved getting dressed up for the dance and her wheelchair did not stop her from getting out on the dance floor. Alyssa could shake her tail feathers just as much as everyone else.

She had a blast at this camp. Alyssa has always kept in touch with the friends she made at camp.

Alyssa also attended Camp Camp in Comfort, Texas, on several occasions. This was another fun camp for Alyssa and a chance to make more friends. It was a camp for children and adults with special needs. The first year Alyssa was at Camp Camp she just loved her counselor (Rin), she always referred to Alyssa as Miss Sassy which I am sure she was. At the end of camp, they passed out awards to all of the special needs children. Rin told Alyssa her award was for being so sassy. We drove six hours each way to take her to this camp, but she enjoyed it immensely. We never thought twice about taking her to camp. We wanted to take advantage of every opportunity available to her.

Alyssa also would attend dances in Tyler, Texas that The ARC of Smith County would host for Special Needs Children. This organization always hosted a dance at Christmas and Valentine's Day. This was always a chance for Alyssa to make new friends and everyone had a great time, you could just see it in the faces of all of the kids.

Our beautiful butterfly always loved being around people, Alyssa was always an extrovert. She was an energetic person, and being around people energized her even more. Though she welcomed opportunities to meet new people, she faithfully kept up with all her friends. Alyssa was a great friend to so many people. She would call people just to see how they were doing, and I know this cheered them up, especially some of her older friends who didn't get many phone calls. She made friends in all age groups, which was a remarkable gift. She was able to find common interests with every one of her friends, regardless of age. Life was good for Alyssa, but she always made others' lives so much richer and better through her zest for living every day to the fullest.

Babysitters were also very special in Alyssa's life. One of her memorable babysitters was Staci. Staci was a volleyball and basketball player in high school and often took care of Alyssa. Alyssa even went with her to many of her games. During their time together, they often played baseball and swam. Alyssa and Stacy even did a cooking show together about Ms. Grammy's Cookies. They made cookies and did a video with the help of Staci's sister, Brandy, and her mother, Lisa. This was so much fun. The sisters played house and did all kinds of fun things with Alyssa. Sometimes they would play restaurant. Stacy would burn the edges of the menus so they would look fancy. Lisa would be the cook, Brandy was the hostess and waitress, and Alyssa and Stacy were the ones being served. Alyssa thought this was such a fun thing to do. She enjoyed cooking and helping out in the kitchen. Entertaining was always the name of the game. Once while riding on our mule/utility vehicle, Alyssa and Stacy ran out of gas. Stacy couldn't leave Alyssa, because they were in the woods. So Alyssa started steering, while Stacy pushed the mule out of the woods. When I saw them, I took them to get gas. One would think they'd be exhausted by then, but they went right back out riding again. Staci was always like a big sister to Alyssa, and they remained friends always. Alyssa was one of her bridesmaids in the wedding when Staci got married a few years ago. Alyssa thought this was very special enjoying going to fittings for the bridesmaid's dresses and getting her hair done the day of the wedding. Staci always made Alyssa feel like she was a part of everything and never left her out of anything.

When Alyssa was younger, I worked part time. Alyssa enjoyed it, because she could come with me. I usually worked while Alyssa was at school, but if she was out for some reason, she wanted to come with me and help. Sometimes Alyssa and Grandma Jane would both come and help out; it was a family affair. I adored having her with me. We always had so much fun with everything we did together, even work.

At the age of twelve, two days after Christmas, we found out Alyssa needed to have yet another surgery. She needed to have Herring rods put into her back to help her sit up straight and prevent her from crushing her organs.

This surgery was a very major yet necessary surgery. The doctors told us Alyssa had a 50/50 chance of surviving the surgery. But if she didn't have the surgery, Alyssa would be gone within a year, because her organs could not survive the strain being placed on them. The surgery was very intense, and she had to stay in the hospital two or three weeks. They cut from her neck all the way down to her tailbone and around her stomach. Alyssa also had to wear a specially made back brace for six months. Through this entire procedure she only took one pain pill when she got home. Alyssa was very strong and never needed the medicine. Daddy Dave and I were always amazed by how well she recovered from these life-threatening surgeries. Alyssa was an extremely strong little girl, and continued to inspire us. Nothing slowed her down for very long. Soon after her recovery, Alyssa was on to another adventure.

As always, Alyssa was ready for a new challenge, so she participated in the Special Olympics in Mabank, San Antonio, and Diboll, Texas. At this time, Alyssa was twelve or thirteen years old. She did wheelchair racing and softball throw. Alyssa was awarded first-place medals in both events. She had a fantastic time at these events and as usual, put all her energy into these activities. Alyssa's aunt Marie, uncle Keith, and uncle Louis were all at the Special Olympics when Alyssa competed in San Antonio. That evening we all went out and celebrated, which she enjoyed to the fullest.

As a result of the spina bifida, Alyssa could never have regular bowel movements without a lot of help. So when she was fifteen, it was surgery time again. This time she had Chait tube surgery, which would help her with this situation. Once again, we saw her strength and endurance. A tube goes through the side of your stomach and into your bowels. It worked well for a while, but the tube kept coming out, which was pretty scary. Whenever it came out, we had only a couple of hours to get it back in or get to the hospital before serious complications would occur. The incision would close, and the doctors would have to do surgery again. It was difficult to get it back in. Once it came out while there was an ice storm outside, and we could not drive into Tyler to get to the doctor. Her daddy Dave called the ambulance to come and pick us up. The Chait tube came out another time when Alyssa was with her grandma Jane and her aunt Annette. Grandma Jane tried to get it back in, and so did Alyssa. It took several tries before it finally went back into position. The problem started occurring much more often, and we realized the Chait tube was not going to work. After about five years, we had it removed and another surgery done that worked much better.

At age sixteen, Alyssa's tonsils and adenoids had to be taken out because of some breathing problems. She was not well for about three days after this surgery. I had to constantly check on Alyssa. It took about one and one-half weeks to recover. The doctor said the older a person is, the more difficult it is to recover from this surgery.

At age seventeen, in December, Alyssa had surgery to have the tendons in her knees released. She was in a cast from her upper thigh to her ankle. She got very sick after this procedure and ended up in ICU with pneumonia. Alyssa was in ICU for four days and in the hospital for eight days. Once again, she was a fighter and recovered as strong as ever. In April of that year, she had another surgery to release the tendons in her hips. Alyssa was in a cast from her waist to right above her knee. While in this cast Alyssa was not able to sit up. During this time Alyssa had a loner wheelchair that would recline so that she did not have to stay in bed the whole six weeks. Our butterfly was determined to go to school and attended every day, lying flat in her wheelchair. She rode the bus during this time, because I couldn't get Alyssa's wheelchair into my van. It didn't matter, she did not want to miss school. She always loved going to school and being with her friends.

When she was eighteen, Alyssa had Lasik surgery on her eyes. She liked this surgery, saying, "It was the best surgery I ever had, because I did not have to wear glasses anymore." Alyssa did great with this surgery, too, and it proved to be very successful. What a great thing it was not to have to wear those glasses. Our beautiful angel was a beautiful young lady with or without glasses. Her beauty was so deep and was both inside and out. It had a glow, as her smile could melt everyone she met!

At eighteen, Alyssa got kidney stones again and had to go to Baylor Hospital in Dallas to have them removed. This was a day surgery, and as always, Alyssa was remarkable in her tolerance and recovery. Nothing ever seemed to slow her down for long.

Along with all of these surgeries, she had numerous other procedures done and had to spend countless hours with doctors on a regular basis. There were usually two or three doctor appointments each week. Alyssa also spent many hours visiting doctors at the Wound Care Center. Alyssa could not feel her feet and would hit them on the dresser or the wheelchair, and a sore would develop. The sores would not heal due to poor circulation, so she had to continue to go to wound care on a weekly basis until they were completely healed. Alyssa took everything in stride. She was such an inspiration to all of us.

Our butterfly had so much pain and trauma in her entire life as she endured all the surgeries, procedures, and doctor visits, but she always fought the fight that only a warrior could fight. And Alyssa always did so with no complaints and always with a smile and zest that were so contagious to all who came in contact with her. Alyssa was well rounded and accomplished in so many areas, and most anything she attacked, she conquered.

One of Alyssa's greatest accomplishments was her graduation from high school. It may seem like a simple task to most, but graduating from high school was a huge accomplishment for Alyssa. She began attending Frankston Jr. High in the sixth grade. Alyssa also went on to graduate from High school. Alyssa loved her years in Frankston schools and made many friends. She was involved in everything: drama club, yearbook staff, FFA, and many other extracurricular activities. All of these groups took many field trips, and she was always at the front of the line ready to go and participate in everything. While in drama class she attended the play *Arsenic Old Lace*. She thought it was the funniest play ever and laughed and laughed.

While in High school Alyssa also went, with her class, to eat at the Medieval Times Restaurant which is in Dallas, Texas. Most people just love this place, but Alyssa really was not all that crazy about eating with her fingers. She would like to have had a fork she told me when she got home. Alyssa did say that she enjoyed the show that was performed. It was an enjoyable outing with her friends. While in FFA, she had gotten two rabbits: Gracie (a Holland Lope) and Roger (a Jersey Wooly). She loved her rabbits and took them to rabbit shows for judging. Alyssa's rabbits always placed well, including a second place at one show and third place at another. In eleventh grade, she went to the Dallas Zoo, which she enjoyed so much, especially with her love for animals. For her senior trip, she went to Six Flags and loved riding all of the rides. The wilder the roller coaster, the more she liked it. She attended her prom and, as always, looked absolutely beautiful and had a fantastic time. Alyssa always did everything she wanted and never felt like she couldn't participate just like any of her classmates.

Alyssa's school friends were important to her. Jennifer and Alyssa met showing rabbits, and they remained friends. Jennifer was Alyssa's best friend, just like a sister. While in high school, Alyssa thoroughly enjoyed going to the Friday night football games with her friends. Her friends, Samantha and Amanda were great about keeping an eye on Alyssa. She always had so much fun with her friends. I was very scared to let her go without me, but she wanted to hang out with her friends. She finally did talk me into leaving her. She always said, "Mom, I will call you if I need you."

Alyssa's classmates accepted and loved her, as she was always such an inspiration to all. Alyssa got a large mum—the biggest one they could make—that she wore to school before homecoming. It had her name down the zebra pattern ribbon. It was as foofoo as it could be done and very extravagant! Alyssa thoroughly enjoyed the Homecoming football game because each Saturday after the homecoming football game, our small town had what we call Square Fair, with a large parade and all kinds of booths. During Alyssa's senior year, she worked one of the booths with her friends to raise money for their senior trip. Going to a parade, having booths for shopping, and many people for Alyssa to talk to and hang out with were great fun for Alyssa.

One of Alyssa's friends from high school, Brittanny Noelle Rodgers, had this to say about her and how much she meant to everyone.

Yours and Dave's love for Alyssa showed through everything you did, and you have no idea how grateful Alyssa is for it. She loves you both so much; I hope you know that. The first time I met Alyssa was after school one day, when I was heading toward my ride to go home. I started to pass by her, and the first words she ever said to me were "Hey you! Come here!" It makes me laugh to think about it. She had wanted me to help her to Nurse Ginger's, and of course I said I would. On the way over, she asked what my name was and what grade I was in. She just talked and talked the whole time. It was like we were lifelong friends instead of strangers. Alyssa continued to amaze me day after day, when she would come up to me, ask me how I was doing, always with a huge smile on her face, no matter what was going on with her. Alyssa was definitely someone who never met a stranger. I remember this one time during school last year, when me and this other girl were getting into fights all the time over me not wanting to be friends with her because of the way she had treated some people. I was in the hallway between classes, talking to Alyssa, when that girl came up and started yelling at me. Alyssa just kept talking to me, completely ignoring her. When she called me a nasty name, Alyssa just calmly backed her chair up and wheeled directly in front of me. She only barely avoided running over the girl's foot, but she effectively cut her off from me. Afterward, when that girl walked off, I looked down and told Alyssa thank you, still trying not to laugh at the shocked expression on the girl's face. The only response I got was Alyssa looking back at the girl and then smiling up at me, where she continued our conversation like nothing had happened. She absolutely refused to believe she did anything to help me then. Even now, I still can't wrap my head around how Alyssa was one person who could have been angry all the time and probably should have been, but *never* was. It didn't matter what she was going through, she always had time for you. She is always smiling and happy. It is absolutely astounding.

Ms. Howerton, I just want you to know how much I admire your daughter. I love her so much.

Alyssa had two nurses while in school, but one became very special to her. Alyssa adored Nurse Ginger. When Alyssa first met Nurse Ginger, they did not get along very well. Alyssa was actually rude to her. Alyssa missed

Nurse Wagley, who had retired. Alyssa was very close to Nurse Wagley and would even visit her at her home. One day she decided to be nice to Nurse Ginger, and I noticed immediately. I asked Alyssa why she suddenly decided to be nice to Nurse Ginger. Alyssa said, "Grandma Jane and I had a talk about it, and Grandma said that it wasn't right for me to treat Nurse Ginger like that." After that, she agreed to give the new nurse a chance, and they became very close. As a result, Alyssa probably ended up being closer to Nurse Ginger than to Nurse Wagley. She inspired Alyssa so much that she wanted to become a nurse. Nurse Ginger wrote the following about Alyssa recently: "I was Alyssa's school nurse, saw her two times every day, and over time, we became buddies."

Ginger Worsham—MISS ALYSSA HOWERTON … lived life to its fullest. Her stature was small, her little legs did not work, but … that did not slow her down one bit. Lyssa embraced life and all it had to offer. She never felt sorry for herself or her limitations and was not one to have a pity party. She would greet each day and live each day as if she were ten feet tall and bulletproof. Forever upbeat and cheerful, Lyssa (Alyssa was sometimes called Lyssa) could talk, text, and email a blue streak, and always had something going on. She never met a stranger, with that warm personality of hers, and she rarely missed a day of school, even with her limitations. She really enjoyed traveling and her exotic animals, which she called her babies. She was very loyal to her friends and family. Oftentimes she would roll into the clinic with a good-smelling candle, some lotion, a card, a picture, or candy for no reason at all. "Thank you, Alyssa, but what is this for?" I'd say, and she'd respond, "Just 'cause I love ya," and she would hug my neck for an hour. Her pic is on my fridge, as seeing her big smile warms my heart. Her life was so enriched, with many wonderful memories that were made, thanks to her endearing mom. I like to think God has a most special place created just for special kids like Alyssa! Keep smiling!

—Ginger Worsham-Voorheese

During Alyssa's high school years, she also participated in many non-school activities. Cheerleading in Texas Stadium: what a blast! Every Sunday was practice. Alyssa and her cheerleading team did a dance routine to the song "Great Balls of Fire" in front of thousands of people. She received a cheerleading trophy for her outstanding performance there. Alyssa got to meet all of the Dallas Cowboy Cheerleaders and take pictures with them. She also performed at a nearby college and received a trophy for her exceptional performance there.

Alyssa enjoyed going to the fair every year and riding the rides. She had to ride the rides with her uncle Carl or her friend Staci, because I could not ride the rides; they would make me sick. Alyssa wanted to ride everything! One year I bought a specific number of tickets and told Alyssa, "Once we use these tickets, we are going home." It was not a popular decision. Every time we turned around, someone was giving us more tickets, and that meant more rides. So much for my ideas! Alyssa also enjoyed playing the games and won Clifford the Big Red Dog one year. This was one of her favorite cartoon shows.

Alyssa even went roller-skating with her Aunt Annette and Uncle Carl. There were several other friends and cousins of Alyssa's at this event. I have pictures of Alyssa out on the skating floor skating around the room. She never sat on the sidelines and watched, but was always involved in the action. She enjoyed participating in every thing.

Our butterfly was ready to travel at the drop of a hat—or a suitcase. Alyssa went with her aunt Annette and aunt Marie to San Antonio and visited the River Walk and, of course, the Alamo. They also went to a mall and did some shopping. Alyssa also played tennis with her aunts. Alyssa didn't sit on the sideline and watch, she played. She was always involved in everything and never fearful.

Alyssa later took a second trip to San Antonio with me, Daddy Dave, and our really good friend Max to SeaWorld to visit with Shamu. Well, at least watch the show. We also visited the River Walk. Other places Alyssa visited included Kings Island, Six Flags, Pensacola, Florida, and Hot Springs, Arkansas. Alyssa was always ready to go, nothing was going to hold her back.

By the time she was a teenager Alyssa enjoyed her electronic devices. She was always on her computer, cell phone, and MP3 player, and Nintendo. Alyssa never left the house without all of them with her. Alyssa had her favorite TV sitcoms and collected many of the DVD's. She had also become quite the eBay expert; that girl could find some deals! Alyssa would spend hours checking eBay and working the deals on it. If I ever told her I didn't think we needed an item, all she had to do was put that little lip out and say, "Pretty please with sugar on top and a hug in the middle." She knew this always got to me, and I could never say no to that.

Alyssa had the opportunity to participate in a J.C. Penney's fashion show one year and thoroughly enjoyed this event. J.C. Penney's and Texas Scottish Rite sponsored this event. J. C. Penney's provided services for Alyssa to get her hair and makeup done. Alyssa thought it was so much fun getting all dolled up. When it was time for the show

Alyssa got very excited. She whirled her chair across the stage and modeled a gorgeous pair of denim jeans and a multi-colored beautiful top with a gray overlay jacket. The announcer would announce what Alyssa was wearing as she showed off the outfit and Alyssa told a little about herself afterwards. Being on stage was a blast for Alyssa. She thought it was great that she got to keep the clothes too. This was another great memory and fun experience for Alyssa.

While Alyssa was a patient at Texas Scottish Rite Hospital the staff worked with the children, as they started getting older, to help them become more independent. They set up a trip for the children to go see a Dallas Stars game at the American Airlines Center in Dallas, Texas. Alyssa met up with everyone at the hospital and they all walked from there to the game, or in Alyssa's case, she wheeled herself there. It was only a couple of blocks from Scottish Rite. They watched the hockey game and afterwards, they all got the experience of taking the Dart Transit (public transportation). The goal was to teach the children to get from place to place without having to depend on someone else all of the time. They took them to this nice restaurant to eat and to order their own meals without the help from family or friends. This was a really great experience for Alyssa and all of the children.

One of Alyssa's all-time favorite singers was Dolly Parton. During the Christmas season of 2009, her daddy Dave gave her an all-expense paid trip to Dollywood. Alyssa had always wanted to go to Dollywood and now she was getting to go. This trip included five-days to Dollywood for me, Alyssa, her grandma Jane, and her grandma Diane. Her favorite things about Dollywood were seeing the shows. Her favorite show was the "Family Reunion." This show included Dolly's two first cousins and her uncle Bill. They got to know Alyssa by name, because she became their biggest fan, always going back to see their show over and over again. She would sing right along with them. Alyssa knew all of the songs word for word. While in Dollywood, Alyssa also won a guitar while playing the game where you toss the rings on the coke bottles. She was thrilled she did this without any help.

One day we drove to Gatlinburg, Tennessee, to Ripley's Believe It or Not, which Alyssa enjoyed very much. We saw the large aquarium, which had many different types of fish. This was an enjoyable trip and a fun day for all. Also, while in Dollywood we went to the Dixie Stampede. She totally loved this. Dolly Parton owned the Stampede, so anything to do with Dolly was at the top of Alyssa's to do list.

We spent a day in Nashville on the return trip. We stayed downtown for the convenience of seeing everything, and we loved walking the strip. Alyssa wanted to hear some good country music, so we went into a restaurant/bar, had dinner, and listened to a great band. She knew most of the songs, and they were happy to play her requests. We all had a fantastic time!

Alyssa went back to Dollywood the following year, the summer of 2010. Again she enjoyed seeing her favorite show "The Family Reunion," and Dolly's relatives remembered Alyssa from the year before. Alyssa adored seeing them again and wanted so much to meet Dolly Parton, but it always seemed like we had just missed her. Either Dolly had just been there or was coming to the park soon after we left.

She also rode some of the rides on this trip with her grandma Jane and aunt Annette. While on one of the faster roller coasters, Alyssa's shoe went flying through the air. She had lost her expensive, custom-made shoe. The ride operator told us they would look for the shoe after the park closed. Sure enough, the next day at lost and found, guess what? They had found the shoe!

Alyssa wanted to plan another trip to Dollywood during the Christmas season, so she could meet Dolly.

This time after leaving Dollywood we went to Savannah, Georgia. This is a fascinating place, and we enjoyed it very much. We toured the city and ate at Paula Deen's restaurant, The Lady and Sons. Alyssa had wanted to go to Savannah for some time, since she also watched Paula Deen on the Food Network with me. She just knew she would get to meet her. While in Savannah, we saw Paula Deen live and the show for *The Real Women of Philadelphia*. Paula's bodyguard saw Alyssa and wanted to make sure she was able to fully see and enjoy the show. So he pushed her down closer to the front. After the show, he came back to where she was sitting and pushed her down to the stage so that she could meet Paula Deen. She even got her autograph. This made her trip to Savannah even more special. I guess Alyssa knew what she was talking about when she said she was going to meet Paula Deen.

In March 2012, at age twenty, Alyssa had a colostomy, which was another major surgery. She stayed in recovery for about three hours and in the hospital for eight days. A special friend, Beth, came to visit Alyssa during this surgery. She would encourage Alyssa and talked with her about her own experiences with having an ileostomy after her colon cancer. Alyssa and Beth were very close. Beth always describes Alyssa as a gift from God: "I do not believe there was anyone who ever met Alyssa who did not have a bond with her in some way. She was truly a gift from God, and she gave love to all she met. Even on grumpy days, her eyes would twinkle and her sunshine came through." Again, Alyssa was very brave and did amazingly well with this surgery. She wanted to have this surgery done, because she knew it would allow her to be more independent. After coming home, she was so proud of herself, because she could change the colostomy bag without any help. Her aunt Annette describes a conversation she had with Alyssa: "How are you doing, Alyssa?" "Fine, guess what? I can change this bag all by myself, it's real easy." She was so special. She was mindful of friends and loved being with people. She had grown into such a beautiful young lady. As with everyone she came in contact with could see, Alyssa had many opportunities and did everything she wanted in life. She had confidence and participated in anything and everything. Nothing held her back despite the fact that she was in a wheelchair. Many of my family and friends tell me I influenced her to have confidence and be strong. When Alyssa was very young, I always told her there wasn't anything she couldn't do. I made sure she had all the opportunities available to her and was able to participate just as anyone else would. We were not just mother/daughter. We were so very much more—best friends, companions, travel partners, and as we always said, sidekicks! I would always tell Alyssa how much I loved her. Then I would ask Alyssa, "How much do you love me?" Alyssa would hold out her arms as wide as she could and say, "This much, Mom."

Our Butterfly Had so Many Interests and Always Tried to Explore Them All

Alyssa always loved the outdoors, especially hunting and fishing. Alyssa and I went Sika deer hunting at the YO Ranch with a group from Dallas. She had her own guide, and he took us out every day. We ate breakfast from 6:00 to 7:00 and went out to hunt from 7:00 a.m. until lunch and back out again late afternoon until dark. We hunted for three or four days. She got a Sika deer the last day of the hunt, and they took many pictures and even a video. Alyssa had the head mounted and a throw made out of the hide. She absolutely loved this trip.

Hunting was one of Alyssa's favorite sports. She did not want to hunt deer near her home, Alyssa just did not think this was as exciting as the exotic hunt. Who could blame her, why hunt in your own back yard when you can go hunt some place lot's more exciting. But she loved exotic hunting. At age fifteen, Alyssa had the opportunity to go hunting in Eau-Claire, Wisconsin. We flew into Minneapolis, Minnesota, and then drove to Eau-Claire. The dogs would track the bears. Alyssa was given a walkie-talkie so that she could keep up with what was happening. It was the day before we were to leave that the dogs treed a bear way back in the woods. We had to take a four-wheeler three or four miles into the woods. Alyssa was then taken piggyback to the spot where the bear was treed. Alyssa sat on Daddy Dave's knee, and he gave her the gun. She put it on her shoulder and aimed. He knew she needed one clean shot and hoped that she wouldn't miss. They were too close to have an angry bear on their hands, and it would have been difficult to run with Alyssa riding piggyback. Fearless, Alyssa got the bear with that one shot, which was a relief to all.

Alyssa continued to enjoy the outdoors a lot and went on a hunting trip to Laguna Visa Ranch in Del Rio, Texas, when she was eighteen. Alyssa wasn't going to pass up the opportunity, although she was running a fever and sick. When she found out she was chosen to attend, there was no holding her back. Alyssa said, "I don't want to stay home and hunt," even though her family owns an eight hundred-acre ranch near Frankston, Texas. "I'm not a regular person, so I don't want to do a regular hunt. I like to do exotic hunting."

It was a fluke that Alyssa got to go on this Ram hunting trip. There was a little boy who got sick and couldn't go, and we got the phone call at the last minute. Alyssa, her grandma Jane, and I went on this hunt. She bagged a Corsican ram, and as always, we had it mounted. Many photos and a video were also taken on this hunt. Grandma Jane always likes to video special events. Bridgett O'Donoghue, who was a cancer survivor, organized the program for this hunt. She does charity work and helps children with disabilities have many opportunities in life. Alyssa even went to a Fifty Calabria shoot in Shreveport, Louisiana, with Daddy Dave and me. Alyssa always loved going to any kind of shoot with Daddy Dave. The Fifty Calabria was fun to watch because Alyssa was fascinated at how large the guns were and how powerful the ammo was. A Fifty Calabria shoot is a long range shooting competition where one can either shoot six hundred or one thousand yards, but a person can shoot both. Alyssa just loved being around all the action. She would shoot targets and skeet periodically and enjoyed it very much. She was always an avid hunter and loved the outdoors, especially on these exotic hunts.

The love of game hunting and handling began when Alyssa was about two years old. She would watch Daddy Dave process deer meat and wanted to help. So he gave her a slab of meat and a butter knife, and Alyssa cut away. This was fun to her, and did not gross her out at all. During her younger years, Daddy Dave, Alyssa, and I would go deer hunting every weekend. I was amazed Alyssa liked hunting, because she was very much a girly girl in so many ways. Alyssa again showed what an amazing person she was with her various interests.

Our butterfly was very proficient at and enjoyed fishing. Alyssa also got the chance to go fishing in Paris, Texas, with a group sponsored by Toby Yoder who enjoyed doing things for special needs children. He was from Paris, Texas and was such a caring man. He just wanted special needs children to have as much fun as possible. He had a ranch with three ponds for all of the children to fish in. They had many other activities, such as making tie-dyed shirts which Alyssa loved. She liked doing this and getting all messy. They also did archery. They were shooting at balloons that were attached to a target. The goal was to hit the balloon and pop it. Alyssa thought it was going to make a really loud noise, so she had me plug her ears while she shot the bow. They also got to see the elk herd that Toby had. The Elk came right up to the fence after Toby got some feed for them. They cooked and served a large lunch for all of the children at the big elk ranch. It was a beautiful place. Alyssa went on these fishing trips every year for about three or four years and always had a great time.

Alyssa and I attended several picnics sponsored by the Make-a-Wish Foundation. They annually would host a special needs picnic in Murchison, Texas. This event was always huge and so very special for all the children and their families! Alyssa was able to attend this great event five or six times. The children went fishing off a big pier in the lake, and they always had a huge hayride for the children and families. And there was always awesome food.

Bowling, golf, tubing, and boating were among the activities that became a part of our butterfly's activities. Alyssa even had her own pink bowling bowl and loved to go to the lanes and bowl. She learned to play golf when she was around twelve years old. Alyssa's uncle Keith took her to play in Austin, and she always had a wonderful time on their outings. Alyssa had her own set of golf clubs, including some that were adapted specifically for her to use with her wheelchair. She always enjoyed tubing and boating. She loved anything outside or with friends and family. If an activity allowed her to be outside, she was always especially ready, willing, and excited. I think she would have stayed outside 24/7 if I had allowed it.

Another part of Alyssa being outside meant caring for and playing with her animals, including some exotics. She had zebras (Zoey, Nevaeh, Zippy, Roxy, and Stripes). Alyssa's plan was to raise baby Zebras. Alyssa also had a kangaroo named (Lefty) which was like having a little brother. He just loved hanging out in her bedroom. Then came the exotic bird (Willy), a monkey (Freddie), and two beautiful horses (Flash and Fantasy). Show-and tell at school always proved to be very interesting with Alyssa in the class. One fun show-and-tell adventure happened when Freddie escaped from his cage. I had told Alyssa whatever you do, do not let Freddie out of his cage. He is very hard to get back in it. What does she do, let's him out for all her friends to play with. He now had freedom he was not going back in for them, so her teacher calls me to ask can you come help us catch Freddie. Off to Alyssa's school I go with sweet tarts (yes the candy). Freddie loved them and would always go in his cage for one. Occasionally, other animals would visit as well. We had a pair of camels with us for about two years (Crooked Nose Clyde and his girlfriend). Of all the exotic animals she had she loved Lefty the most. She bottle feed him when he was a baby and would put a diaper on him when he was in the house. I guess you could say he was like her baby.

Alyssa always had many normal pets as well and spent many hours with them. Her dog Biskit was with her for ten years; he was a German shepherd and was always very protective of Alyssa. We never had to worry about someone trying to break into our house. Biskit made sure of this. Alyssa's dog Biskit got really sick with cancer right before Christmas 2011 and had to be put to sleep. She was so sad; he was like a brother since she had no brother's or sisters. Alyssa wanted him cremated so she could keep him in her room close to her. Then came Fritz. He was a shih tzu that seemed to love to claw and shred our sheets. Always in the mix were rabbits, fish, and hamsters. Daddy Dave has for years raised and trained national-level trial dogs, and Alyssa was always right there, ready to help train and care for these spectacular animals in any way possible. At one point one of these beautiful animals, Ultra, had puppies. Daddy Dave had slept with Ultra the night before the arrival of the puppies. The next day, the veterinarian was summoned to assist in the delivery, and Ultra gave birth to five beautiful puppies. Alyssa was there to help me bottle-feed the five puppies, although they had to eat every two hours. Alyssa and I even had to assist the puppies go potty prior to each weigh-in. She enjoyed this so much it was like taking care of a baby for her.

When Alyssa was about five or six years old her teacher Mrs. Pat at Children's Place Day Care gave her a cat.

Alyssa named her cat Mrs. Pat after her special teacher whom she adored. We have some of the cutest pictures of Alyssa and Mrs. Pat, the cat. Alyssa couldn't keep her cat at our house, because of our German shepherd dogs, so Alyssa ask her Grandma Jane if she would keep Mrs. Pat for her. Of course, Grandma said yes. Every time Alyssa went over to Grandma Jane's house she had a lot of fun playing with her cat. After graduating from high school, Alyssa met her teacher Mrs. Pat again when she was taking classes at the East Texas Center for Independent Living. Alyssa had the opportunity to have Mrs. Pat for one of her teachers again at this school.

On to the next animal. After coming home from an Alabama trip Alyssa took with her Grandma Jane and Aunt Annette Alyssa got the idea that she wanted fish. While visiting her cousin Sheena she was fascinated with her fish. We thought maybe a small gold fish bowl. Oh no, it had to be a nice big tank with angel fish. So we got a male and a female angel fish thinking we could raise fish. This didn't happen, we could not keep them alive. So the fish tank went to her cousin's Spencer and Sienna. So now we had to try one more inside pet. This time it was a mini hamster. Alyssa named her Lucy, she lasted about 3 days. One day Alyssa comes wheeling that wheelchair into the room so fast, saying, "Lucy is dead Mom". I said, "I think maybe she is just sleeping. "No Mom, she is dead". She was right, she was dead. Off to the pet store we go again to replace Lucy. Alyssa picks a male this time and she names him Jake. Things were going well with Jake until one morning and we could not find him. I thought for sure I would find him dead somewhere, but three days later there he was in a small trash can still alive. We were not sure how he survived with no water or food. Alyssa and I thought it was time to give Jake to Uncle Carl. We took a break from inside pets. I think we were meant to have larger animals.

It was always such a thrill for her cousins to come over and see all of Alyssa's animals. Alyssa had such a love for animals. So many of these moments with her animals were very special and contributed to her becoming the beautiful, compassionate, and well-rounded person she became.

Our Butterfly Loved Parties (Any Kind, Anywhere) and Holiday Events

$\mathcal{I}f$ there was a party or holiday event, my Alyssa was always happy to help plan it. Everything from birthday parties, Christmas parties, school parties, or holiday or special events were great, and she was there. Her favorite part was opening the presents. Alyssa always wanted to open all our presents at birthdays and Christmas. She didn't care what was in the present as much as she loved to open the gifts. Every family event was a party.

Alyssa went to wedding showers, baby showers, and birthdays. But nothing could quite top her birthday parties. Her first birthday party was the weekend before her birthday because of pending surgery on her actual birthday. At her first party, we had a cake with clowns all over it. All her friends and family were there. She got tons of presents, and all the guests stayed late. Some of her friends even helped me give her a bath to get her ready for bed. For Alyssa's second birthday party, she had a Barney cake, and the party was held at Aunt Annette's place. Raggedy Ann was the theme for the third birthday, and Daddy Dave cooked hotdogs and hamburgers for everyone. Everyone played in the pool all afternoon. Uncle Mike dressed up as a clown and brought balloons and entertained the attendees. After those first three, she always had big birthday parties at Chuck E. Cheese, Kids' Depot, or Fire Mountain. Alyssa picked the place, and the planning began at least two months in advance. The kids who attended always had so much fun. They played until they were so tired they could hardly move.

As Alyssa got older, the parties were always swim parties at our home. Her friends from school and family would all be here. When Alyssa turned eighteen, Daddy Dave and I sent a bouquet of flowers to school. Receiving flowers at school was an extreme highlight for this very special time in her life.

Although birthday parties had been such a highlight her entire life, school events were also a highlight. Her eighth-grade graduation was very special. Alyssa wheeled across the stage and received her accolades along with her classmates. About this same time, Alyssa attended her first dance, and she insisted that she go alone. Although very nervous, I agreed to her wishes. I drove her there but left as she had requested. It was a long few hours for me, but it was so very important for Alyssa.

Alyssa's high school graduation party had to be the best ever. Daddy Dave and I had a pavilion built by the pool in our backyard, and it had to be completed by graduation. The pavilion is about 13,000 square feet and is complete with lights, fans, a large counter, and a grill. The party was incredible, just out of this world. Alyssa graduated on a Friday night, and we held the party Saturday afternoon and evening because her cousin Chris graduated the same night Alyssa wanted to go to his graduation party. She had requested a cookie cake for all the guests, as well as all

kinds of grilled food for her family and friends. Our friend
Will was our chef for the day, and we really kept him
busy grilling everything you can imagine eating. Alyssa
received a ton of presents and enjoyed opening them all,
along with being able to host her friends. As always at
Alyssa's parties everyone stayed all day, swimming, eating,
playing various games, and visiting with her.

Our butterfly's visits to Alabama were often the backdrop
for many kinds of parties. Family reunions were always
fun, with lots of food and singing. Sometimes, the parties
were family events other than reunions. At Aunt Lena's
eightieth birthday party, Alyssa sang several songs with
the microphone and had a blast. She always enjoyed the
opportunity to visit with her cousins Judy, Sharon, and
Vivian. Being able to see and visit her aunt Margie and
aunt Lena was a must on every trip. Riding in cousin
Sheena's new SUV was a blast to be had. Being in the
SUV with cousin Sheena made her feel all grown up and
she enjoyed that. Her uncle Jerome's girlfriend Martha
soon became a favorite because she was Alan Jackson's first
cousin and Alyssa just loved Alan Jackson's music. Uncle
Jerome took Alyssa to the Little Brown Church in eastern
Alabama. The church is one hundred years old and has
some Civil War graves in the tiny graveyard. They would
act as though they were having full church services, and
Uncle Jerome was the preacher. While there, the song

"Little Brown Church in the Vale" came on the radio, and we all started singing and having a grand old time. Alyssa always enjoyed visiting with her uncle Jerome.

Not only did our butterfly enjoy her parties, she was also totally involved in helping plan and host parties for family and friends. Uncle Richard's fortieth birthday party was a main event. It was a lot of fun and a surprise for Richard. My fortieth birthday party was at our house. It was fantastic due to the planning of Alyssa and Aunt Annette. They wanted to make it special, and it was complete with balloons and chocolate mousse cake, along with many party guests and a lot of food. We once had a surprise party for Daddy Dave that included a crawfish boil. In preparation for his party, Alyssa helped me plan and cook for days. She was always in the middle of getting everything ready. Daddy Dave, Alyssa, and I hosted a party for Uncle Carl at our house when he turned fifty, and as always, a great time was had by everyone—especially our party girl. Laughter, great food, and Alyssa's touch and planning were always a big part of these parties.

Grandma Jane and Pawpaw Larry's twenty-fifth anniversary was the best. Alyssa helped decorate our large office near our house, and she and Uncle Carl prepared and ran the slide show for this event. They did a great job with the planning and with their slide show. Alyssa had a blast telling her uncle Carl how he was supposed to do everything for the slideshow. When Grandma Jane turned seventy, Aunt Annette was visiting from Arizona, because Grandma Jane had just had surgery on her legs. Alyssa and Aunt Annette helped take care of Grandma Jane and prepare meals for her while she took it easy after the surgery. Aunt Annette and Alyssa took Grandma Jane out to the Cracker Barrel for breakfast one morning. They enjoy going out for breakfast. While there, Alyssa bought Grandma Jane an Alan Jackson CD. She pretended she was buying it for herself, and she wanted Grandma Jane to help her pick it out. Once she bought it, she handed it to Grandma and said, "This is for your birthday." She was always doing sweet things like that.

Aunt Annette and Alyssa thought it would be nice to surprise Grandma Jane for her seventieth birthday. We actually surprised her twice. We began at the Olive Garden, with the family all there for lunch. It was followed by everyone coming back to Grandma's house for cake, beautiful roses, and a special video that included all of Grandma Jane's family. Alyssa really wanted to buy some Silly String for Grandma Jane's party. Alyssa told me, "I pinky swear this is all I want to buy for Grandma Jane's party." Alyssa, her cousins (especially Cousin Isaiah), and Grandma Jane had a blast with the Silly String. Our butterfly had Silly String all over herself. She also assisted with fitting Grandma Jane with a sash and a pink hat. This certainly allowed her to be styling to a very high degree.

Halloween was always so much fun at our house. Alyssa never cared to eat the candy, but she loved to dress up and be taken out to collect the goodies. She had a different costume each year. One year Daddy Dave and Alyssa were cows. Every year we went trick-or-treating at Grandma Diane and Pawpaw Rick's house. Uncle Mike and his friends would always take Alyssa to trick-or-treat through the nearby neighborhood. The Halloween carnival at the church with Grandma Jane always had lots of games and sometimes even a hayride. Of course Alyssa was not going to be left out.

I always planned an annual Easter egg hunt. We would fill up about five hundred eggs with candy, complete with five special prize eggs. The special prize eggs would be filled with money and candy. Then Uncle Richard, Uncle Barry, and several others would hide the eggs on the Saturday before Easter. All of Alyssa's cousins (Spencer, Sienna, Isaiah, and Priscilla)—younger and older (Ryan, Bridgett, Chris, Cory and Cassi) and of course Alyssa were not ever going to miss out on hunting the eggs. They were all hoping to find one of the prize eggs. Regardless, they all went home with a basketfull of candy. Uncle Carl was always Alyssa's egg hunting partner, pushing her wheelchair through the grass so Alyssa could find the eggs. They became very proficient in their hunt. Later, on Easter Sunday afternoon, we would have an Easter dinner with Grandma Diane and Pawpaw Rick.

Mother's Day and Father's Day were always special for us. Daddy Dave, Alyssa, Grandma Jane, Pawpaw Larry, Grandma Diane, Pawpaw Rick, and I would always have dinner at our house, and we had a blast. Grandma Diane always helped Alyssa pick out the Mother's Day gift for me, and the gifts were always so thoughtful and special. Alyssa just loved Mother's Day and so did I. I could never spend too much time with my baby girl.

As great as all the parties and events were, Christmas was always the best. Christmas was Alyssa's favorite holiday, and it always showed in her anticipation and actions. She continued to believe in Santa (even after she was grown, as far as we ever knew) and would never let anyone build a fire in the fireplace on Christmas Eve, because Santa might be burned. When Alyssa was little, we would make reindeer food and sprinkle it outside for the reindeer, and she would put cookies and milk out for Santa. Alyssa and I always put up our tree the day after Thanksgiving. It had to be the big tree; a smaller tree would never do. Daddy Dave put the lights on the tree, and Alyssa and I decorated it together, which Alyssa loved. I began putting gifts under the tree two weeks before Christmas, and she checked every day to see if there was a new one. On Christmas Eve, Santa came and put his gifts for Alyssa under the tree. Christmas morning, Alyssa always got up early and opened her many, many presents.

After having Christmas at home, we went over to Grandma Diane and Pawpaw Rick's for more Christmas activities. Daddy Dave, Alyssa, and I always went there on Christmas Eve as well as later in the day on Christmas. Going to her Grandma Diane's for Christmas Eve and Christmas Day was always one of the highlights of the Christmas season and the year. One thing Alyssa particularly enjoyed during our visits there at Christmas was singing "Old Susanna" while Grandma played the keyboard. Grandma Diane always went over the top at Christmas for Alyssa. Diane always got special gifts for her and made a special Christmas dinner with the most delicious food you've ever had. On Christmas Day at Grandma Diane and Pawpaw Rick's, we would have snacks, open presents, and hang out together. Later came that oh so special Christmas dinner that Grandma Diane would always make.

Sometimes we did Christmas the day after at Grandma Jane's. We sometimes would have a treasure hunt for the younger children, which they loved so much. For the adults, we would play Dirty Santa. Dirty Santa is a game where every one brings a gift and then we draw numbers to see who picks the first gift. If the person that picks second likes what number one picked that person can take their gift or pick from under the Christmas tree. As the children got older, they also played Dirty Santa. It is a fun game! Alyssa loved Christmas and being at Grandma Jane's. She enjoyed being with her big extended family. Alyssa was such a giving person; she wanted to buy for everyone. All through her school years she bought gifts for all of her teachers, nurses, friends and family. She just wanted to be sure everyone had as good of a Christmas as she did.

Alyssa loved seeing the Christmas lights at Santa Land, and our family waited in line one year for three and one-half hours to see the lights there. It was worth it to Alyssa; she would have waited all night. The Christmas season was very important to Alyssa, and if she had her way, Christmas would be year-round.

Our Social Butterfly Saw Many Medical Professionals

Some of the most important people in Alyssa's life were her doctors, nurses, and therapists. They were like angels to her, helping in so many ways. Alyssa and I were grateful for all their help throughout the years. Dr. Hargrove was Alyssa's pediatrician until she was nineteen years old. He first met Alyssa when she was born. She once told him that she wasn't leaving his office until he retired from being a doctor. She loved all of her doctors but was especially attached to Dr. Tom Hargrove. His office also did picnics for special needs children at Camp Tyler every spring, and we always attended. Alyssa got to dunk Dr. Hargrove in the dunking booth at one of the picnics. Alyssa thought this was the best thing ever. She waited in line just to have the chance to dunk him. Sure enough Alyssa threw the ball right at the spot to make Dr. Hargrove fall into the water. She joked with him about this for a long time. Boy, did she love that! Dr Hargrove was a fantastic doctor and such a good sport. Dr. Hargrove told me he always used Alyssa as a positive example to other patients, even though he could not use her name. Alyssa had made such a positive impact on him. He says it best in his own words.

"Hearing her say, "Hargrove!" I would hear this from the hall or an exam room, and I knew right away my day was going to be a little more interesting and a little more fun. Alyssa would not let you get off easy if you were [perhaps] a couple of minutes behind in your schedule. She had "spunk"—enough of it to spread around to those she knew and loved, and "shy" was not in her vocabulary. I might try to kid around with Alyssa, but she was always ready to give it back. As I watched Alyssa grow from a baby to an energetic young adult, I was so inspired by her refusal to allow her disability to limit her. Although she might have had times she felt physically bad, she would bounce back and be on to her next adventure or achievement. Supported by her loving and devoted family, Alyssa overcame and accomplished much. Alyssa's story is an incredible motivation to me as I care for patients. She shows that physical limitations can't get in the way of love, compassion, attitude, activity, and enjoying life. I'll never have another patient like her, but her example is one I will use to live and to help with the healing of others for many years".

Alyssa saw Dr. Merritt for her foot. It was dropping downward, so Dr. Merritt would give her a Botox shot in her calf, which helped a great deal. She loved Dr. Merritt so much and would cut up with him. He also prescribed physical therapy for her. At first, they had therapists come to the house twice a week to do therapy with Alyssa. As she got older, we went to the therapist's office three times a week—Monday, Wednesday, and Friday. Alyssa did not like going to the therapist's and sometimes begged me to let her skip, but it really helped her with her upper-body strength.

Dr. Scardina was Alyssa's psychiatrist. She started seeing him when she was about nine years old. He kept her calm, and they would chitchat about what she'd been doing and how things were going. Most children with a disability deal with depression. Fortunately, Alyssa didn't have a serious problem with depression. She did take the medicine prescribed for her ADD.

Dr. Scardina thought it might be beneficial for Alyssa to talk with a counselor to give a different point of view on some issues in life. She started going to see Dr. Peggy Baldwin every other week. Dr. Baldwin was young, and Alyssa could relate to her a lot. She was a wonderful counselor. They would talk for an hour alone unless Alyssa needed me to explain something. Dr. Baldwin was someone Alyssa could chat with about personal things. Alyssa enjoyed the visits and became close to her counselor. She went to see her for two years, once every two weeks. I usually went shopping, and she would call me after an hour to come and pick her up.

Dr. Valdez was Alyssa's wound care doctor. Oh my, Alyssa loved this doctor. He had a baby who had been born prematurely and had a hole in his heart. He would go to Dallas every week to see his baby in the hospital. He would show Alyssa pictures of his baby, and she was very concerned about the child. Alyssa could relate to this very much and always wanted an update on his child. The doctor and nurses at wound care were fantastic and went above and beyond for Alyssa. If she had a wound, Alyssa would go weekly until it was completely healed. Alyssa got wounds easily, because she could not feel her legs, so we did spend a great deal of time at wound care.

Dr. Ellis was Alyssa's family doctor and saw her for the last nine months. Dr. Ellis was a very caring doctor and came to the hospital when she was ill. She wanted to see Alyssa every three months to do blood work and check on her. Although Alyssa didn't want to give up seeing Dr. Hargrove, he had gone into administrative work at the hospital. Alyssa was beginning to form a bond with Dr. Ellis.

Dr. Rippy was Alyssa's gynecologist, whom she saw once a year. She also gave Alyssa her depo shot once every three months to help with her cramps. Alyssa loved this doctor and could really relate to her. Our butterfly always asked for the shot in her leg, since she couldn't feel it there. Alyssa enjoyed joking with the nurses at Dr. Hargrove's office very much. Alyssa had them all wrapped around her finger. Anytime Alyssa needed anything and I called, the doctor or nurse always called me right back or they gave me a back line to get them right away. Alyssa and I are very thankful for all of the wonderful medical staff we have been privileged to have throughout the years.

Alyssa spent a great deal of time at Children's Medical Center in Dallas as well as Texas Scottish Rite Hospital in Dallas. These hospitals are incredible places for children. They have many wonderful specialists there and an unbelievable staff of medical professionals. Alyssa became friends with the doctors and nurses there as well as just being a patient. The volunteers were wonderful also. They came by the children's room daily and let each child pick a gift off the gift cart. These hospitals have life skills areas, where the children could go down to play. We always enjoyed our time there greatly. In the life skills area, they had games, books, and movies for the children. This was a place for children to get out of their hospital environment for a little while and was always such a blessing.

ALYSSA

Family and Family Friends Were Always so Important to Alyssa

Aunt Annette "Alyssa is like a daughter to me and I love her with all of my heart. I enjoy spending time with her; she makes me laugh with that great sense of humor of hers. Sometimes I tend to take life too seriously. . I remember one time when Alyssa was going through her root beer phase, we were shopping at Wal-Mart and Alyssa wanted a root beer. I bought her a root beer and I ask her if I could have a sip. After taking a sip, I let out the loudest belch and she laughed and I laughed. We were both laughing so hard. She thought it was hilarious, because belching in public just wasn't something Aunt Annette did. Every time we went to Wal-Mart she always wanted a root beer, but from that day forward she always wanted me to drink part of it. We always had so many good laughs together, sometimes we laughed so hard that we were crying. Although I live in Arizona we are very close. Alyssa would flutter over to Arizona and spend time with me as often as she could. At age three, Alyssa came for a visit, and we went skiing with family and friends at the Sunrise Ski Resort in northern Arizona. She wanted to be involved in everything. What energy she had. I remember one hot summer day in Phoenix we spent many hours at Castles and Coasters, riding all of the rides. The hot sun didn't seem to bother her. We usually went to the mall and out for lunch, which was always fun. Yes, Alyssa did go to the Grand Canyon on one of her visits to see me. 'Wow, what a *big* hole,' she remarked. We toured the canyon and later went to the I-Max Theater and saw the *Grand Canyon Show,* which was spectacular. We went to Sedona, Arizona, too. It is a beautiful place, with all the red rocks. While there, she saw Nicholas Cage's house, which she was interested in very much. We also went to Jerome, Prescott, and Flagstaff, Arizona. Like her aunt Annette Alyssa enjoyed traveling. Alyssa, you have taught me so much. I love you always and forever."

Alyssa is smiling from ear to ear so happy because her aunt Annette is here. She may live in Arizona, but she comes back often and spends most of her time with my dear Alyssa. Alyssa loved her aunt Annette. They'd go shopping and probably buy another 2,000-piece puzzle. Oh, how she loved those puzzles! Cooking? Yes, she always wanted to help with the whole process. She could make some pretty tasty lasagna. They usually cooked when they were at Grandma Jane's. They would clean and organize her kitchen, too. Organizing spices was not beyond her realm of talents. Painting, puzzles, photos, and home movies were favorite pastimes for them. Just spending time together was what they enjoyed most, just laughing, joking, and being together. Alyssa was a fun person to hang out with and always happy.

Boy, did they both love to be on the go. I remember all of those Alabama trips to see the relatives. This was Alyssa's favorite of all her travels with Grandma Jane and Aunt Annette. Sometimes they would go on shorter trips to Austin and San Antonio, too.

Aunt Marie Alyssa enjoyed visiting Aunt Marie and Uncle Louis in Austin. After Aunt Marie moved back from Arizona onto Texas soil, she never missed a birthday and spent many Christmases and other holidays together. Aunt Marie states: "I treasure all of our times we had together. Just being in the same room was comforting, and holding Alyssa's hand, just because she felt like it, and her heartfelt hugs. Some of my fondest memories are going to movies, shopping, having French toast Uncle Louis made for us (nearly every visit), the first time we took a plane trip to Arizona together and just hanging out. I will miss all her little ways—when Alyssa was happy and even not so happy. I always felt like she could talk to me. Not only was she my niece but my friend. There will always be a special place in my heart for Alyssa Brooke Howerton. It will be where the butterflies like to hang out … you know, when you get those fluttering feelings, that's where."

Uncle Carl "Alyssa looked at people in a different light; she was nonjudgmental and loved and accepted everyone. She had tons of reasons to be depressed but wasn't. She had the greatest personality and was so outgoing. She would get me to do things I normally wouldn't do because of shyness, but Alyssa helped get me out of my shell. It is amazing how much I learned from Alyssa. She was never a burden but always a blessing. I never looked at her as handicapped!"

Uncle Carl was always here to take care of Alyssa when we were gone. They did everything together. They would hang out and eat junk food. Uncle Carl even once took Alyssa to a special needs wedding. They went to Wal-Mart and out to eat. He was her hangout buddy when Daddy Dave and I were out of town.

Uncle Barry was another one of Alyssa's special uncles that seemed to always be at her graduations and other important events in her life. Sometimes he might miss some of our family gatherings, but Barry some how always managed to be there for Alyssa's special moments. He is a very loving, caring and compassionate uncle and Alyssa loves him very much.

Uncle Keith "Going to Tyler for us always consisted of us first stopping by Frankston to see Alyssa. She was always a handful and certainly a good debater. Don't know that we ever won a debate or argument with Alyssa. I guess the best thing about visiting—other than the free room and board (tasty food); skeet shooting contests; zebra, horses, and other exotic animal viewings; and Jacuzzi sitting were the big hugs she always insisted on giving and receiving right before we left to go home. Those will be what we remember the most."

Uncle Scott has always enjoyed spending time with Alyssa, too. She even spent time with Scott and his buddies during his high school years, when Alyssa was younger. They would talk, and she was always involved in their discussions, no matter what they talked about. Later, she always wanted to spend as much time as possible with Uncle Scott, Aunt Dominique, and Cousin Ava.

Beth Adair "Years ago there was a Barry Manilow song that kept coming to my mind the first day of Alyssa's life. As I was with her at Children's Medical Center-Dallas,

I was singing to her … 'Sweet Alyssa [It is Melissa, but I changed it for her.], Angel of my life time, Answer to all answers I can find … Baby I love you Come, Come, Come into my arms Let me know the wonder of all of you.' It might sound like an odd tune to sing to a baby, but she had so much in her to give from the moment she was born, and I wanted to be part of that. All my time with her was spent in a hospital room, but not at any time did she ever feel sorry for herself, and she always allowed me the 'wonder of all of you' feeling. I am truly blessed to have been with her. I hoped that my words on her first day of life would sink into her very soul and she would show the world what an incredible gift life is to all of us. I miss her, but she is deep in my being, and I find myself smiling because of her."

Cindy Armstrong "Marlena, I am a good friend of Di and Rick's. I worked for Rick at Snelling for eleven years. I was honored to give Alyssa a book I wrote *Boudreaux and His Buddies.* I got to spend a little time with her when she was at Rick and Di's. I was passing through from New Orleans to Dallas. I remember how sweet she was and how much she made me laugh. Such a kind and giving spirit she had. I met you once, when you came into Snelling with Alyssa and she was just a little girl. You had her in your arms. My heart is sad for you and David. No matter how old they get, they are always your baby, and I know you had an even deeper bond because of how much you had to care for her. I know that caring for her was a privilege for you. She came here in her condition for a reason. She had the unique capability of blessing others with her kind presence. You are special to have been picked as her mom. She was here to show you what real love is. Be confident that you did the best you could do, and you gave Alyssa a wonderful life full of love, laughter, and lots of animals for her to enjoy."

Jack and Denise "We were so blessed to be given the privilege to get to know such an awesome young lady as Alyssa. Her smile, her beauty, and her charm were extraordinary. But even that paled by comparison to the charm and grace she always showed to everyone. She was truly one of the strongest people we have ever been blessed to know. She made an unbelievable impression on us. She loved with a passion not even capable by most! She lived with a zest most would never even comprehend. She was truly a blessing."

Gina Smith Ellis "Even though we didn't get to spend a great deal of time with Alyssa, she was very much a part of our lives. This is a sweet little story for your book. When Alyssa was about seven, she met Johnathan, and she insisted on singing a song to him—the whole song [that Barney made famous] 'You Are Special.' She sat and held his hand, and sang to him like she had known him all her life. It meant so much to Johnathan. We have spoken of that time often through the years, and it just shows the depth of love in Alyssa's heart and makes us understand and appreciate humanity more than we ever would have without her. Alyssa inspired us to be more loving and kind to our fellow neighbors and that is a big deal."

Our Butterfly and Her Daddy Dave Teaching her to Fly

Daddy Dave always loved to spend time with Alyssa. Daddy Dave was so patient with her. He taught her everything from shooting a gun to working on remote control cars and planes. They would spend the evening in the hobby shop, working on their cars and planes and just talking. After putting in many hours on a new plane, it was finally time to see them fly, and they enjoyed taking them to the office for a flight. Our office has a nice big landing strip for the radio controlled planes they built. Not only did Daddy Dave fly remote planes, he was a pilot. Alyssa was able to accompany him to the Reklaw Flyin at the Flyin M Ranch in Reklaw, Texas.

Another of Daddy Dave's hobbies was working with clay. Daddy Dave and Alyssa made the Washington Monument out of clay for a school project.

Most of all, they would make sure that the animals were all feed. He always had a hard time feeding the babies. Alyssa and I would pick up the slack. Daddy Dave shared his love for animals, especially dogs, with Alyssa. She so enjoyed going to the Shutzhund Trials.

With so much to do on our place, a four-wheeler was the best vehicle for the job. Of course, Alyssa would be right there to ride and help regardless of the task. She loved to ride the four- wheeler. One of her favorite foods was grilled cheese, but only if Daddy Dave would make her his "World Famous Grill Cheese." No one made them like Daddy Dave!

Daddy Dave had another tradition he had started with Alyssa on Sunday mornings. He had bought her a high-tech waffle maker, because he knew how much she loved waffles. Alyssa thought Daddy Dave made the best waffles in the world. After the work was done, the best way to relax was hanging in the pool with Daddy Dave and me. She was always ready to hang out with us at the pool.

Our Butterfly Was Compassionate and Loved with a Passion

Alyssa was the most compassionate person I've ever known. She felt the pain of those hurting. If you were sick, she would hold your hand and comfort you. For example, when her grandpa Rick was sick and in the hospital, she stayed with him all day and held his hand rather than go shopping with me. She was very concerned about him. She was always concerned about anyone not feeling well. On one trip back to Alabama, at her Uncle Lonvell's funeral, she pushed her wheelchair from one family member to the next, hugging and comforting them. If I was sad or down, she would always comfort me. She understood pain and was able to empathize with others in a very genuine way. She was encouraging and concerned for all. She always asked how they were doing. She loved all people and didn't like it if someone was being negative toward another person. She set the perfect example by just being herself. She didn't complain or feel sorry for herself because she was in a wheelchair. Rather, she enjoyed life to the fullest every day.

Try to imagine having to cath each time you needed to go to the restroom and having to fill three or four syringes of warm water and inserting them into your body just to have a potty. Imagine being in a wheelchair all day long every day. Just think how exhausting that would be. Getting up in the morning and having to take about fifteen pills before the day started. What about having to continue to have surgeries and go to doctors routinely due to infections or sores that would appear out of the blue. She took everything in stride. She was the most amazing person I have ever known, and I'm not just saying this because she is my daughter. She never complained, yet she was thankful for her life. I asked her from time to time if it bothered her to be in a wheelchair. She said, "No, it doesn't bother me. I can do anything anyone else can do." She did, too. She was such an inspiration to me and made my life so rich and full.

Alyssa meant the world to Grandma Jane

<u>Grandma Jane</u> "From the time Alyssa was born we spent many precious hours together. She always enjoyed coming to my house. She loved to organize my canned food, taking it all out and putting it back into the cabinet again. She also would organize my video tapes and photos. How she enjoyed looking at photos of all of our family and friends. We both enjoyed our classic country and gospel

music. We had the same taste in music despite our age difference and we always enjoyed singing together. I will always treasure all of the hours I spent with Alyssa whether it be the fun times or our times in the hospital. We had some sad moments, but we had many laughs together. I will always remember Alyssa's enthusiasm and joy she had for life and how much she loved people. It is hard to believe that she is gone, I sure miss her beautiful smile and big hugs. Our hearts are so sad and it hurts so much. I look forward to getting to see Alyssa and other loved ones again someday. One thing that gives me hope and peace is knowing that this is not goodbye, but it's until we meet again."

Alyssa loved babies. She enjoyed taking care of her younger cousins and was there when her cousin Spencer was born. She was going to be there and watch the birth, but her aunt Marie had to have a cesarean at the last moment, and the doctors wouldn't let her stay for that. She always enjoyed watching the "baby channel," as she called it. It would show the entire birth of a baby. She would change cousin Spencer and her cousin Sienna's diapers. If she saw a baby when she was out in public, Alyssa always wheeled up to meet the baby and asked questions about it. Sometimes people would let her hold their baby, which was what she wanted most.

Alyssa was extremely good with babies, too. She told me if she ever had a little girl, she would name her Gracie Nevaeh. She liked the name Nevaeh, because it was heaven spelled backward. She liked the name Gracie, because she felt like she was here by the grace of God. Alyssa truly was a gift from God.

We just found out that Uncle Keith & Aunt Zhen are having a baby. They waited to tell everyone, because they knew it would upset me. I did get upset, but only because I know this little cousin will never get to know Alyssa and what a strong, loving person she was. Alyssa loved babies so much, I know she would have wanted to just hug and cuddle the new baby when it arrives.

During Alyssa's life, she met many people, and so many told me they were inspired by the life she lived. Unfortunately, she passed away on May 15, 2012. It was a shock and happened very quickly. She got a gallstone, which caused an infection that took over her kidneys and liver. The infection got into her blood and went septic.

At Alyssa's funeral, uncles wore purple shirts, and her aunts and I wore purple dresses in her memory. Purple has been her favorite color since she was very young. Other family members wore purple, too. We wore corsages made up with purple flowers and a butterfly in each. She loved butterflies, too. She always liked the singer Dolly Parton and saw butterflies in Dollywood. Her room was decorated with two large, colorful butterflies. Some of the family wore zebra-patterned clothes, because Alyssa loved her zebras. I know Alyssa would have liked this much better than everyone wearing all black. We also had a friend put together a slide show with pictures of Alyssa throughout the years and her favorite music. This played throughout the service.

This has been the most difficult thing I've ever experienced in my life, and I don't think I will ever get over it. Alyssa was my life, and I don't know what I'm supposed to do now. My days were always full with her and my routine was with her. And I've been lost since she left me. Alyssa was my life, and now I just go through the motions each day, not knowing what to do. I wish someone would tell me what I should do now. Alyssa usually had a couple of doctor's appointments each week. I took her to school/classes, and afterward, Alyssa and I would go out to eat. Sometimes we would get pizza and watch a movie together. There was never a day that we did not tell each other "I love you." Every morning when I went to help Alyssa into her wheelchair, we sat on the edge of the bed and hugged and told each other how much we loved each other. Alyssa and I were as close as we could be without being the same person. Alyssa wasn't just my daughter; she was my best friend. Many blessing come our way in life, but I sincerely believe the blessing I was given was the greatest of them all. This angel that was sent to me encouraged and blessed our lives and the lives of all she came in contact with. All my family is devastated by our loss. Alyssa was the center of our family. We are all filled with sorrow and pain. As a friend once said, "She truly was all the proof of God's love that anyone could ever need." We just don't understand why he took her from us at such a young age. She was such a blessing, and I just wish I could see her again and give her a hug and kiss. I have had so many people tell me after the first year things will be easier, others have told me it will take two years. I am thinking that it will never be that easy for me. I will go on, but I will always keep her memory alive. I miss my daughter more with every day that passes. As I look back on my daughter's short life, I know that Alyssa had a life most would dream of. Alyssa had the chance to do more than many people that live to be eighty or ninety years old. If her body would have allowed her to do it she was sure going to try. I wish everyone could see life through a Special Needs Child's eyes. Daddy Dave and I will always remember how much Alyssa touched everyone she ever came in contact with. Alyssa gave me a beautiful poem one Mother's Day that means so much to me. It is called

"M-O-T-H-E-R"

written by Temple Bailey. This poem is about a Mother's love and all of the things that she does for her child. This poem touched my heart and is so special to me, because it is from Alyssa. This poem is something I will always treasure. If you have never read this poem please look it up it is a great poem.

Alyssa was my baby and so special to me. One thing I do know is that Alyssa was the greatest blessing I've ever been given. I have experienced the richest love possible as a result of having Alyssa. She has been the best daughter a mother could ever want, perfect in every way. When I think of my daughter Alyssa. I think of her kindness, warmth and her strength. I will always be her mom. Alyssa was deserving of all things good. Alyssa was one of a kind. I could have another baby, but this would not replace my Alyssa. I cry every day and probably always will. Not a day will pass as long as I live that I do not think about my little girl.

Each year we are having a celebration in memory of Alyssa's inspiring life. This is something we plan to do each year on or around Alyssa's birthday. At this first celebration we invited Alyssa's family and friends. We had a cookie cake which was always Alyssa's favorite. We also released twenty-one balloons in her memory. Also friends and family made a donation to the East Texas Center for Independent Living in memory of Alyssa. This got started when Uncle Scott wanted to make a donation to an organization in Alyssa's name. Daddy Dave and I thought it would be good to make the donation to the East Texas Center for Independent Living since Alyssa took classes there after high school which she enjoyed immensely. She made some very special friends there. She took cooking classes which she loved. Alyssa also took math, and reading classes. Things she especially enjoyed was planting herbs. She grew chives and enjoyed watching them grow. Alyssa wanted to grow herbs, because she knew I enjoyed cooking and that I was always using different herbs in my dishes.

For more information or to make a donations to East Texas Center for Independent Living call 903-581-7542 or write 4713 Troup Hwy, Tyler, Texas 75703

I Lost my best friend now. You might have died too young, but your memory lives on. I know I can't bring back yesterday, but Lord can you help me find my way...

I can still see you sitting next to me Singing and Shaking your head to the music.

Do you realize what you've done touched the hearts of everyone.

It just isn't the same since you left our world. I know I can't bring you back, and the only thing that gets me through is knowing we'll all be together again someday.

Our Final Words to Our Precious Daughter, Alyssa

You will always be in our hearts. We love you so very much. You are our life. We're not sure how we are going to get past this, but I know you're saying, "Momma, don't cry." I always told you, Alyssa, I'm trying not to. Just looking at your pictures makes us so happy. Your smile just lights up our day. Your uncle Keith is sitting by me and wanted to say he painted his nails purple just for you (hands and toes). He is also using your ice pack. Hope that's okay.

We know you can see just how many hearts you touched. Everyone loved you so very much, but you were not only our daughter but my best friend, my whole life. We will miss you more than words can say. We know you were so tired of being poked and know you're resting now. But our pain is so bad right now. Please help us, baby girl, to just get through the day. You're everywhere we look. We don't want to be selfish, and we know you're safe and taken care of now. Alyssa you always said, "Momma doesn't do it that way!" We always did as much as we could for you and just wanted you to have a happy life. You sure made our lives happy! Momma will always miss my little sidekick, and Daddy Dave will miss his little helper and buddy.

Love you always, Mom, Daddy Dave and Your Best Friend

Daddy Dave & I both got purple butterfly tattoos with your name and birthday, so we will always have a part of you with us. God only knows how we miss you. The only thing that gets me through is knowing we will see you again someday.

The following quote expresses my feelings at this very moment for my baby.

"If tears could build a stairway and memories a lane, I'd walk right up to heaven and bring you home again".

From a Friend

A friend of mine gave me a poem/story about the symbolism of the Butterfly. Since Alyssa loved butterflies so much I thought I would give the Title and Author. I hope you will take the time to read this.

The Symbol Of The Butterfly - By: Nola Gypsy Vodou

"The next time you see a butterfly, I hope you'll take the time to watch it as it flies, for The butterfly has come to bring you a message and give you peace and love in your journey.

It has been a little over five months since my daughter Alyssa passed away. I had a dream about her the other night. In my dream Alyssa came to me as I was working in our flower beds in the back yard. I looked up and Alyssa was sitting in her wheelchair and I ask her if there really was a Heaven. Alyssa replied, "yes Mom". So I ask her then why are you still in your wheelchair? Alyssa told me, "when I am in heaven everything and everyone is perfect". "For me to come back and let you know that I am ok I had to come back the way I left". Alyssa gave me a big hug and a kiss. I ask her when I would see her again and she said, "when you come to Heaven".

My Book is Dedicated to

My daughter Alyssa Brooke Howerton.

Special Thanks

Thank you, to all of my family and friends for all the wonderful things they had to say about my daughter and for encouraging me to tell my daughters story.

Thanks most of all to Alyssa's Daddy Dave for all his love and support through this very difficult time. I also want to thank my Mom and Dad Jane & Larry Kepler, and Mother and Father-in-law Diane & Rick Greene you all mean so much to me. And my two sisters Annette Coffey and Marie Hunt for all their help and support, (and extra thank you to my sister Annette for all her help with my book), also thanks to all my brothers Jerome, Carl, Barry, Richard Keith and Mike Coffey and brother-in-law Scott Greene, and all of my sister-in-law's. I would love to mention everyone's name but the list would go on forever.

Alyssa Brook Howerton

August 31, 1991 – May 15, 2012

We thought of you with love today,
but that is nothing new
We thought about you yesterday,
and the days before that too.
We think of you in silence,
we often speak your name.
All we have are memories,
and your pictures in a frame.
Your memory is our keepsake,
for which we will never part.
God has you in his keeping,
and we have you in our hearts.
A million times we wanted you,
a million times we cried.
It broke our hearts to loose you,
but you didnt go alone,
For a part of us went with you,
the day God called you home.

I love you Alyssa,
Rest in Peace,
My beautiful friend